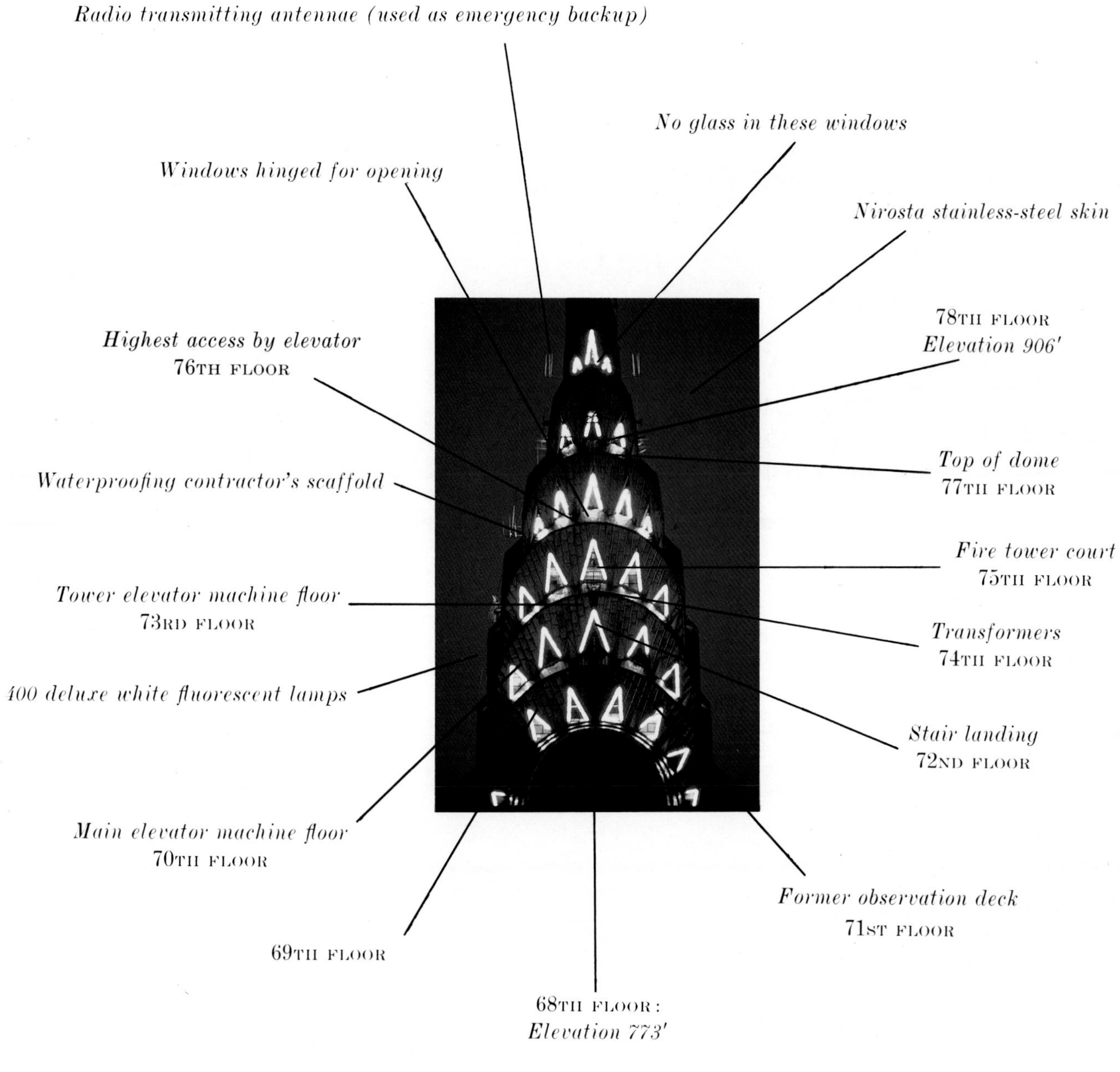

Radio transmitting antennae (used as emergency backup)

No glass in these windows

Windows hinged for opening

Nirosta stainless-steel skin

Highest access by elevator
76TH FLOOR

78TH FLOOR
Elevation 906'

Waterproofing contractor's scaffold

Top of dome
77TH FLOOR

Fire tower court
75TH FLOOR

Tower elevator machine floor
73RD FLOOR

Transformers
74TH FLOOR

400 deluxe white fluorescent lamps

Stair landing
72ND FLOOR

Main elevator machine floor
70TH FLOOR

Former observation deck
71ST FLOOR

69TH FLOOR

68TH FLOOR:
Elevation 773'

The Top (Almost) of the Chrysler Building

When the Chrysler Building was completed in 1930, the 904' 11½" dome was high enough to make it the world's tallest, a title held since 1913 by the Woolworth Building. During construction, some Wall Street p.r. men claimed a building planned at 40 Wall would be taller. Architect William Van Alen went back to the drawing board and came up with a 141' stainless steel spear, which was assembled inside the dome and shoved up through a hole in the roof to bring the building's height up to 1047'. The title of tallest remained at the corner of 42nd Street and Lexington Avenue until the Empire State Building topped out at 1472' in 1931. (Don Hamerman)

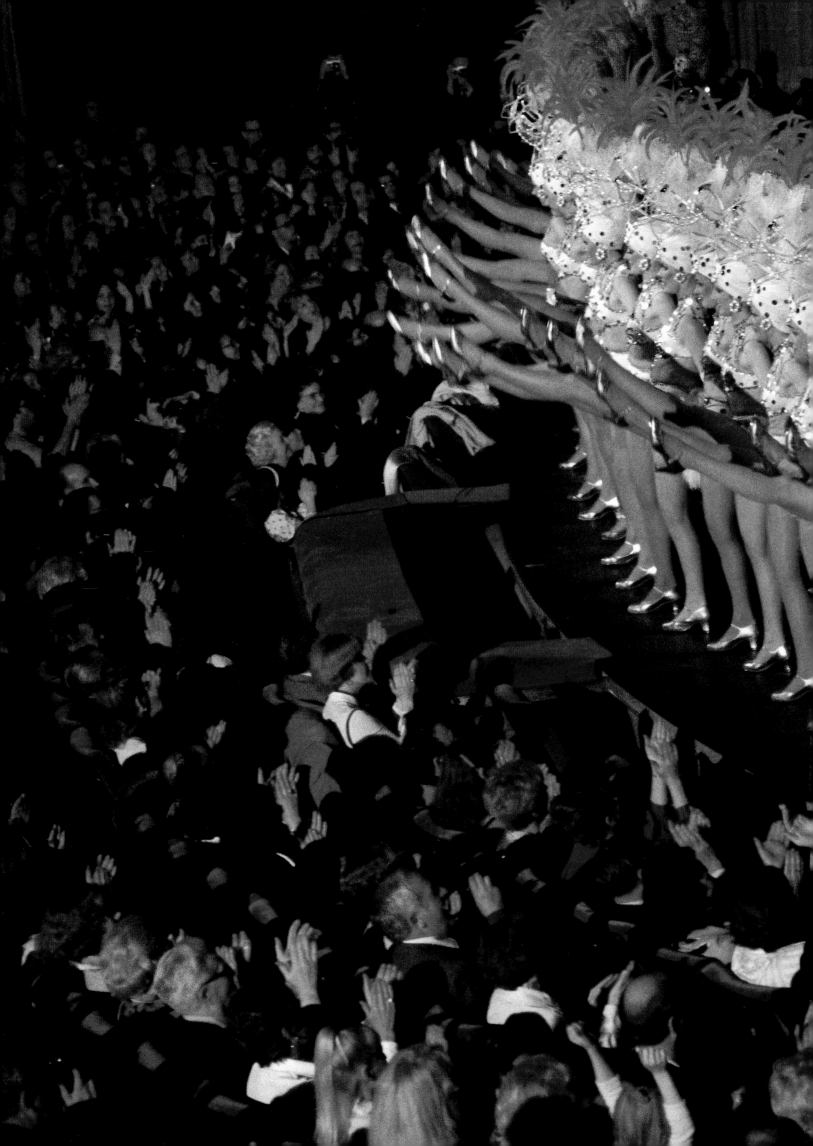

NEW YORK AT NIGHT

BY BILL HARRIS

INTRODUCTION BY J.C. SUARES

STEWART, TABORI & CHANG PUBLISHERS
NEW YORK

Design: J. C. Suarès
Editorial consultant:
  Marya Dalrymple
Photo Editor: Don Hamerman
Research: Roberta Newman
Production: Caroline Ginesi

Published in 1983 by Stewart, Tabori & Chang, Publishers, Inc., New York. All rights reserved. No part of the contents of this book may be reproduced by any means without the written permission of the publisher.

Library of Congress Cataloging in Publication Data
Harris, Bill 1933–
    New York at night.

1. New York (N.Y.)—Social life and customs—Pictorial works. 2. New York (N.Y.)—Description—Views.
I. Title
F128.37.H37   1983
974.7'1043'0222
83-7998
ISBN 0-941434-38-9

Distributed by Workman Publishing, 1 West 39th Street, New York, New York 10018

The text was set in Devinne and Futura Light by U.S. Lithograph Inc., New York, New York.

Printed and bound in Japan by Toppan Printing Company, Ltd., Tokyo, Japan.

In 1979, Radio City Music Hall threatened to close forever. It didn't; the Rockettes are still kicking up their heels. (Sonia Moskowitz)

Though the Brooklyn Bridge has hardly changed since opening in 1883, the neighborhood near it has. The South Street Seaport restoration will bring 1883 back. (Dan Lecca)

A hired carriage makes its way down Fifth Avenue from 59th Street and Central Park. (Don Hamerman).

Thomas Edison himself brought electric lights to New York in 1882, and his company, Con Edison, has been lighting the way every since. (Chuck Dorris)

Russell Baker once wrote in the Times that "The girls of New York, like the girls of Paris, are for watching and making the city inexplicably more exciting." (Martin Schreiber/Black Star)

The best time to fly into New York is just after the sun sets, when the downtown skyline gives you its warmest welcome. (Marvin Newman)

New York's 9,000 professional fire-fighters respond to over 111,000 fire alarms a year. (Andrew Holbrooke)

Who doesn't love New York? On nights when the Goodyear blimp is here, it passes so close to the World Trade Center observation deck that you can almost touch it. (Chuck Dorris)

CONTENTS

ON THE TOWN

"I'M BORED WITH NEW YORK," SHE SAYS.

It's 9 P.M., she's ready to call it a night, and it's upsetting her. She keeps talking about other places, places where the nightlife is wildly elegant. She says, "You must come to Caracas. You will be my guest. New York is dead at night." She looks through the revolving doors of the Mayfair Regent toward an empty East 65th Street and sighs. "Dead. Dead. Dead."

She's the richest woman in South America, maybe the world, and she's not ready to listen to reason. She never listens to anybody, not to her servants, not to other rich people, not to her fifth husband, and certainly not to me. So there's no choice but to pack her, her diamonds, her ivory cigarette holder, and the rest of her essentials into the back of the red Rolls waiting outside and give her the grand tour of the city. By the end of the night she should be convinced that for sheer variety of entertainment there is no place like New York at night.

Outside, Maximilian, the chauffeur from the limousine service, is shining his shoes in the right front seat. He has one foot on the dashboard, and he is applying black polish to his shoe with a steady, circular motion. He looks up, not exactly delighted to see us. Just then, a dented yellow Checker cab races by. The driver slows down briefly to negotiate a huge pothole the size of the Sea of Tranquillity and simultaneously throws his empty paper coffee cup out the window. The cup sails down the street and lands in front of the Rolls. My friend, looking disgusted, says "New York is not only boring, it's filthy. Filthy, filthy, filthy."

Well, I think, the night is young. I'll show the lady from Caracas what New York nightlife is really all about and she'll forgive the little things like rude drivers and garbage. She arranges herself in the back seat and peers out the window with an expression not unlike that of someone stranded in a lifeboat surrounded by sharks and barracudas. "We will go to the best place," she commands. "You do know the best place, yes?" I explain that the *New York Times* pretty much decides which are the best places, but I give her a quick restaurant rundown, assuming she's hungry.

Off the top of my head, I tell her that in Manhattan alone, there are 286 Chinese restaurants, 187 Italian, 86 French, 68 Japanese, 20 Korean, 18 Mexican, and 2—both called Sammy's —Rumanian. There are five four-star restaurants in the city, among them Lutèce and La Grenouille, both French, where you can expect to dine as well as you might in Paris—if that's what you want. There are a few non-French four-star places; one, Hatsu- hana, a Japanese establishment on 48th Street between Madi- son and Fifth, serves the best sushi in town. After that there are 17 three-star restaurants, 82 two-star, 140 one-star, and plenty with no stars at all. Restaurant owners live in terror of opening the paper one day to find that they have received a bad review

It's illegal to drink alcoholic beverages on the street in New York, and drinking in a car is an even more serious offense. Often the law looks the other way, but that must have been hard to do in this case. (Jean Pigozzi)

PREVIOUS PAGE
You can now drink champagne 'til 4 A.M. every night at the Odeon, a former cafeteria on West Broadway in TriBeCa. (Karen Kent)

or that they have just lost a star or two. Then there are the establishments that just keep packing them in, stars or not. Sardi's on 44th Street and Joanna's on 18th might have been rated "fair," but they're filled to capacity every night. Who cares if the veal scallopine tastes like an old sneaker when you might see Lauren Bacall at the next table or Richard Burton at the bar?

There is one restaurateur, however, who doesn't care about reviews or reviewers. In fact, not long ago he refused to serve the *Times* critic and even went so far as to throw her out. His name is Buzzee O'Keefe, and he owns the River Café. I tell my friend this story and she immediately says, "I like this Buddy O'Keefe. We will go to the River Café."

The Café is on a barge attached to a dock in Brooklyn, beneath the Brooklyn Bridge. It took O'Keefe nearly ten years to get it going before it opened in 1977. First there were bureaucratic problems, then technical ones. The critics found the food adequate; but the public found the atmosphere and the view of Manhattan irresistible; and the restaurant was a success from the moment it opened.

The limousine looks beautiful on the Brooklyn Bridge, or maybe it's the Brooklyn Bridge that looks great with the limousine on it. We reach the Café and find that every table has been reserved. She shrugs. "So. It is too early for supper." But we decide to have a drink on the patio anyway. The view is breathtaking; traffic on the bridge above sounds like a million bees gone berserk.

My lady from Caracas sits in judgment, scrutinizing the crowd. There are too many tourists on the patio for her taste. I'm beginning to understand what she finds amusing. She'd rather be dressed to the nines in silks and diamonds and feathers, joining a happy, frenzied bunch of natives dancing in the streets. I say forget it. New York is not Rio. We don't dance in the streets. We sit at bars or in restaurants for hours and hours. Or we may go dancing, but only on dance floors. And we dance very self-consciously because we don't have any native dances or anything like what they do all night in South America. She says, "I do not understand how you can go to a bar and sit there just drinking." It's very simple, I explain. Happiness to a New Yorker is sitting at a bar and having the bartender—your bartender—serve you your drink before you've had a chance to order it. It's a common ritual, something that one comes to expect. A real bar-goer has one bar, one bartender, and one favorite drink. So if you're looking for a bar, I tell her, look for one with only one bartender. Two-bartender bars are not quite as cozy. And three bartenders means a drink factory, pandemonium, a total lack of communication.

My favorite one-bartender bars are the 23rd Street Bar & Grill, the Carlyle Hotel, the Tavern on the Green, the Palm, the Ginger Man, Le Relais, and One Fifth Avenue. There are some great two-bartender bars, like Martell's, P. J. Clarke's, and the Plaza's

OVERLEAF
For some, a late-night debutante's ball can be an excursion into fantasy land. Others find it a hoot. (Charles Harbutt, Archive)

ORIGINAL NASSAU BAR AND GRILL
Three barmaids

JIM McMULLEN
No stars

222 EAST 35TH STREET
No doormen

MARTELL'S
Two bartenders

LA PETITE MARMITE
One star

944 PARK AVENUE
One doorman

LANDMARK TAVERN
One bartender

PALM TOO
Two stars

BERKSHIRE PLACE
Two doormen

THE PALM
Three stars

THE PLAZA
Three doormen

LUTÈCE
Four stars

(All photographs: Don Hamerman)

NICHOLAS
One limousine

OREN AND ORETSKY
Two limousines

HOEXTER'S MARKET
Three limousines

THE WALDORF-ASTORIA
Four limousines

THE 21 CLUB
Five limousines

Oak Room; but I can think of only one three-bartender bar I like. It's the Riviera in Greenwich Village. Her eyes are starting to light up.

We're back in the Rolls at ten minutes to eleven. I'm hungry, but she doesn't respond to my appeal to find a restaurant. She wants to drive around and see where people hang out. "Where *is* everybody tonight?" Simple, I explain. Just count the limousines in front of a place and it'll tell you something. There are one-, two-, three-,four-, on up to twelve or more limousine places. Now I'm sorry I ever mentioned limousines. She has found a game to play—count the limousines. She tells Maximilian to slow down every time we come to a cluster of cars; then she counts out loud like a referee! "Oren and Oretsky's, two limousines. Maxwell's Plum, six. Tavern on the Green, seven. Hoexter's, three limousines. The Plaza has ten . Ah, Nicholas has only one. The Palm, nine. The 21 Club, five." She's driving Maximilian and me to the brink of madness. And I'm starving.

Still, something wonderful is going on. As the night wears on, my companion is getting more and more excited, and she is beginning to look radiant, even years younger. She's smiling. By midnight she is finally at home in New York. It looks as if I'm going to convince her that she has come to the right place.

At quarter to one she says, "Let's go dancing," and I give up supper for good. We're on Park Avenue; and now she's decided to count doormen. The least elegant buildings have one. Quite a few have two. Then she notices one with three. "Somebody just paid eight million bucks for a 12-room apartment in this building," volunteers Maximilian, "and they almost didn't let him in because he owns tankers. No guarantee that he's always going to be in the money." She just keeps counting—anything that comes

THE PLAZA
Ten limousines

up—as we search for a place to dance. She passes on Regine's, Xenon, the Red Parrot, Danceteria. Suddenly, out of the blue, she says, "I know the best place. It's the Reggae Lounge." I've never heard of it and neither has Maximilian; so we ask a cabbie, then head for TriBeCa.

At the Reggae Lounge a huge bouncer runs a metal detector up and down my legs and then motions us both in. "This is *the* place to dance. They talk about it EVERYWHERE!" She's right. The music is great. We move with the crowd to the delirious beat of reggae. No one is trying to show off. Reggae doesn't permit pretentiousness.

By 2 A.M. she is even more alert. She has met some friends from Rome on the dance floor and they're talking about moving on to the Continental. By the time we arrive, everyone's wired. For me, sitting on the balcony overlooking the dance floor is like flipping through old issues of *Photoplay*. There are celebrities here from every decade since the talkies were invented. Just as I think I'm going to faint from hunger, she announces that she's ready for supper. She says, "Let's find an outdoor café. I want to watch people go by." This is fine by me, so I suggest a sidewalk table at the Empire Diner.

Near the corner of 22nd and Tenth, the Empire is undoubtedly the most elegant diner in the world. It is open all night, every night, except for a few hours on Monday morning. As we feast on caviar omelettes and asparagus, we watch the dawn break. It looks as though someone has set fire to New Jersey.

I'm hoping that she'll ask me if the Empire Diner is the only restaurant open all night, then I can recite my litany of open-all-night places to her. She finally bites and I casually begin. You can get a pizza at Charlies' Pizza; you can eat with the cabbies at the Market Diner; you can have a filet mignon at the Brasserie. There are three Burger Kings open all night and a dozen Chinese restaurants, several bagel places, at least two dozen luncheonettes and delis. You can even have falafel at 5 A.M. at Mamoun's Falafal on MacDougal Street—and that's just in Manhattan, I tell her. "I'm full," she says.

It's 7:00 A.M. and Maximilian is snoring in the front seat of the Rolls. My friend from Caracas takes one look at him and says "Let him sleep. You will take me home in the subway. I have never taken the New York subway. Never. Never. Never." I don't believe this.

A little later we are sitting exhausted in a graffiti-painted car, heading uptown on the IRT. Our evening clothes are a sharp contrast with the coveralls and hard hats that a couple of Con Ed workers sitting next to us are wearing. They are oblivious to us as they head for their jobs, but the minute they look up, the lady nods and smiles. "I think New York is divine," she says to one of them. My back aches, but I haven't felt so good in months. "Tonight," she says, "you will show me more." And I realize that I've done it. She's sold on New York at night.   —J. C. Suares

Peter Beard and a few friends sit one out at Studio 54. (Sonia Moskowitz)

An opening at the O.K. Harris art gallery in SoHo. (Jean Pigozzi)

IN JANUARY 1886, THE BISHOP OF THE METHODIST
Episcopal Church in New York City called a press conference. He
stunned his audience by announcing that there were more prostitutes
in the city than there were Methodists.

Not long after, the superintendent of police, in a press conference of his own, confessed he didn't know anything about Methodists.
But he asserted that there were only 3300 women engaged in sex-
for-pay at the 621 brothels and 99 hotels that specialized in
assignations. He added that over 700 of the total 3300 were "waiter
girls" in dance halls and saloons, and they, at best, should be classified as semiprofessional. He neglected to say where he got his fig-
ures or why his minions weren't doing anything about it.

The bishop had put the number at 20,000. But he and the superintendent were probably both wrong. Wickedness had hit the city
like a plague in the years after the Civil War. Before 1861, when
the war began, most of the vice in the city was confined to the East
River waterfront south of Canal Street, where the girls who walked
such streets as Bowery and Water were known as "night walkers."
By the time the war ended, there was so much competition in that
area that the girls began moving into other parts of the city; and
because they also began appearing in the daytime, they picked up
a new name: "street walkers." The neighborhood many of the
prostitutes found most attractive, an area bounded by 14th and
42nd Streets and Fourth and Seventh Avenues, was called "the
Tenderloin," so-named in 1876 by a police captain who said, when
he was transferred there, that he was pleased to finally be eligible
for a little tenderloin after all those years of chuck steak.

Just outside the Tenderloin, a row of seven houses on West 25th
Street east of Eighth Avenue contained the most famous brothels
of the era. They were known as "The Seven Sisters"—no relation
to the well-known group of women's colleges—and all operated
under the same rules: patrons were required to wear evening clothes
and often to bring flowers to the girls. None of the well-heeled
customers considered this a hardship: the Grand Opera House was
just around the corner at 23rd and Eighth, and the men had to get
dressed up to take their wives there anyway. They were grateful
to have a place to slip away to while the opera was in progress.

But if elegance and culture thrived on Eighth Avenue in the
1880s, neither word was heard much over on Sixth Avenue. The
stretch of Sixth from 24th to 30th Streets, where the wholesale
flower district is today, was the part of the Tenderloin known in
every part of the United States as "Satan's Circus."

In those days, before there was a Brooklyn Bridge or a Statue of
Liberty, the city's top tourist attraction was a dive at the corner of
30th and Sixth known as the Haymarket. Any traveling business-
man who found his way there probably never forgot the experience.
In the daytime, the Haymarket looked like an abandoned building;
but at night, all three floors were ablaze with light, and a barker
out front did his best to fill the place for what was called the
grande soirée dansant. Women didn't have to pay to get in, but

men were charged 25¢. Once inside, drinks for ladies cost 20¢ apiece, while a gentleman could get one cocktail for 15¢, two for a quarter (the difference was based on the fact that women got a brass token with every drink, redeemable for cash at the end of the night).

The Haymarket had originally been a theater, and conversion didn't change it much. The stage was kept intact, as were the boxes and galleries. For an extra fee, usually 50¢, a patron would be shown to a table in one of the boxes, where he could watch the dancing on the floor below—that is, if he could cut through the cigar smoke. But the real show took place in little cubicles installed behind the boxes, where the extra fee bought a private demonstration of a new dance sensation called the cancan.

The Haymarket stayed open for over 40 years until Prohibition killed it in 1920, which says a lot about the value of the tourist business. Even more popular with the natives were such places as the French Madame's, named for its owner, a woman who weighed in at more than 200 pounds, sported a small mustache, and doubled as the bouncer. Don Kerrigan, owner of the Strand, another popular place nearby, was one of a list of saloonkeepers with interesting avocations: during the day he was an important Tammany Hall committeeman. The saloonkeepers were able to bring in a lot of votes, and many of them did very well with the Tammany organization. Tom Foley, who operated out of his saloon near the criminal court building in lower Manhattan, was so successful that Foley Square was named in his honor.

Though Satan's Circus was a focal point of New York night life in the second half of the nineteenth century, it was far from the only scene of action. Up and down the Bowery there were places known as concert saloons, which purported to provide entertainment along with the drinking. The heaviest drinker in the place usually turned out to be the entertainer—always a piano player who was always known as "The Professor." It didn't matter that he was often too drunk to play the piano, or whether he knew how to play at all; most of the patrons were just there to drink anyway.

Some of the Lower East Side saloons did provide more solid entertainment in the form of Punch and Judy shows, and often the "waiter girls" would lift their skirts and attempt to dance. Boxing matches were also popular, and it was at a concert saloon, Harry Hill's on West Houston Street, where the great John L. Sullivan made his New York debut in 1881.

But the best fights of all were among the patrons themselves. Sudden death was commonplace; maiming, routine. A newspaperman from Cincinnati told his readers of a place on Hester Street: "There is beastliness and depravity under this roof compared with which no chapter in the world's history is equal."

So-called respectable New Yorkers knew the perils that lurked on the Lower East Side and had begun avoiding the area as early as 1850, even though in those days the Bowery was the heart of the Theater District. By 1860 a newspaper noted: "Actresses too corrupt and dissolute to play elsewhere appear on the boards at the

Frank C. Henderson and his wife,
among other revelers, toast New
Year 1939 at the St. Moritz Hotel.
(The New York Daily News*)*

Bowery.... Newsboys, street-sweepers, rag-pickers, begging girls, collectors of cinders fill the galleries of these corrupt places of amusement." Nevertheless, there were still about 100 theaters going strong on the Bowery at the turn of the century.

The class acts were at places like Wallack's Theatre, Niblo's Garden, and Barnum's Museum on Broadway at the edge of the neighborhood called SoHo today. In 1854, when the Academy of Music began presenting Italian opera on 14th Street at Irving Place, the action began to move uptown, beginning with theaters that presented minstrel shows. In 1860 Wallack's Theatre moved up Broadway to 13th Street, and the drama world never looked back downtown.

Though producers did all they could to lure "respectable" patrons with such rules as refusing to sell tickets to unescorted women, they weren't above providing a little titillation. One show that was all the rage in the mid-1860s was *The Black Crook*, and it included a cast of 100 women whose legs were bare to just above the knee. It shocked Mark Twain, who said the show was "nothing but a wilderness of girls dressed with a meagerness that would make a parasol blush." Charles Dickens said it was "the most preposterous peg to hang ballets on that was ever seen." But the *Tribune*, which called it "rubbish," had to admit "All that gold and silver and gems and light and women's beauty can contribute to fascinate the eye and charm the senses." The show ran for 475 performances and earned a profit of $1,100,000 before it closed at the end of 1867.

Night after night the rich and influential flocked to the Union Square neighborhood to be entertained and enlightened at such places as the Academy of Music. But the "new rich," including the Vanderbilts and the Goulds, resented having to sit in orchestra seats to hear opera at the Academy while "Old Money," represented by such families as the Astors, the Delanos, and the de Forests, looked down on them from the 18 private boxes. The new rich proposed the addition of 26 new boxes. When the management refused, a group of these new millionaires bought a piece of property on Broadway at 39th Street and began building their own opera house. The building, which opened in October 1883, had plenty of room—122 boxes arrayed in three tiers. The old aristocracy stayed put on 14th Street, however, and the competition between the two opera houses gave New York the most glittering season this or any other city has seen before or since. An Italian critic wrote: "The public has had the luck to hear in a single winter all the living celebrities in the world, a luxury certainly not afforded by any capital in Europe." But the city could not then support two operas. The following season the Academy of Music closed its doors forever, and the Metropolitan Opera became the only place to be seen.

The Academy's closing marked the end of the Union Square area as a theater center. The move uptown had already begun in 1869 when Edwin Booth opened a theater he named for himself at Sixth Avenue and 23rd Street, and by 1886 the Metropolitan Opera

In October 1961, the big attraction in the Times Square area was a place called the Peppermint Lounge, where (nearly) everybody did the Twist. (Wide World)

In 1935, the Savoy in Harlem was a place to be seen. The entertainment and dancing were the tops. (Aaron Siskind)

At Studio 54, the general rule for dancers is "Look but don't touch." It's a rule that's occasionally broken. (William Coupon)

House had lured enough theaters uptown to make the new Rialto the stretch of Broadway from 23rd to 42nd Streets.

But if the climate on 14th Street wasn't good for show business any longer, the restaurants in the neighborhood went right on thriving. In the early evening hours it was still tough to get a table on the terrace at Brubacher's Wine Garden, facing Union Square, or at Muschenheim's Arena, which had one of the best wine cellars in town. But more fun than any of them was the former Mehlbeck's Beer Hall, bought in 1882 by young August Luchow with money provided by his friend William Steinway, who owned a piano factory around the corner. Steinway used the place as a base for entertaining important clients and visiting artists, and he never failed to appear each day for the special 45¢ lunch. Luchow enjoyed the place more than anyone, though, and most evenings he would consume three or four dishes from the menu and wash it all down with beer drunk from a custom-made six-quart stein. In addition to clearing tables and pouring water, the busboys were charged with carrying Luchow upstairs to his apartment when he'd had enough. It took four of them.

Luchow's Restaurant didn't suffer at all when the Academy of Music closed. In fact, it stayed at the same location for exactly 100 years before moving uptown. Old Money didn't suffer much, either. Carrie Astor had decided that being seen in a box at the opera wasn't enough to mark someone as an important member of Society, so she began holding an annual ball at her Fifth Avenue mansion (presently the site of the Empire State Building). Since the capacity of her ballroom was 400 persons, it was simply understood that the 400 she invited were the only real Acceptable Society in town. Though social arbiters believed that this was true, there were spoilsports in New York who thought they could buy status by holding their own lavish banquets in one of the hotels and restaurants around town.

Chief among these restaurants was Delmonico's on William Street. Here, in 1865, an English tea merchant started the one-upmanship with Mrs. Astor by entertaining 100 influential citizens at a dinner party that cost him $200 a plate. In 1873, Lorenzo Delmonico was asked by Edward Luckemeyer to provide "the most memorable dinner in history." He constructed a lake in the center of his restaurant, surrounded it with trees and flowers, and stocked it with swans imported from Prospect Park in Brooklyn. Even more outlandish was a dinner party held at Sherry's on Fifth Avenue at 44th Street. The formally dressed guests dined on horseback in the brilliantly decorated, thickly carpeted room. The food was served on trays that were attached to their saddles; champagne was kept chilled in ice buckets concealed in their saddlebags.

Out-of-towners got a chance to rub elbows with upwardly mobile socialites at the Brevoort Hotel, built in 1854 at the corner of Fifth Avenue and 8th Street. But rubbing elbows became a fine art when the Fifth Avenue Hotel opened in 1859 on the corner of 23rd Street. In 1860, Edward, Prince of Wales, stayed there and

Anyone who wants to feel the true spirit of New York at night needs to spend some time in Times Square. Like the rest of New York, it's in a constant state of change; but nevertheless, the spirit is there. The pictures on the following pages were taken in the Times Square neighborhood by Marvin Newman in 1954. His intention was to capture the mood of the people he found there—like the girl in the car in front of the Whelan Drug Store on 42nd Street near Eighth Avenue. But he also captured the setting, which has almost entirely vanished over the years ... The Camel Cigarettes sign that blew smoke rings at passersby from the front of the Claridge Hotel on Broadway between 43rd and 44th streets (unnoticed by these formally dressed patrons of the Astor Hotel across the street) ...The Kleenex sign on the roof of Toffenetti's Restaurant (now Nathan's) on 43rd, with its neon version of "Little Lulu" demonstrating the product's pop-up box and trying to catch the attention of a pair of visiting paratroopers ...The stained glass windows on the second floor of the Broadway-near-46th Automat, now a Burger King ... The low-priced eateries with who-knows-what upstairs ...The street-corner preachers with their American flags.

Times Square had other special attractions in 1954. There were 73 productions on Broadway that year, including Josephine Hull in Solid Gold Cadillac, Deborah Kerr in Tea and Sympathy, Tallulah Bankhead in Dear Charles. There was a revival of On Your Toes with Vera Zorina; Carol Haney was dancing in Pajama Game; and over on Sixth Avenue, Alfred Drake was the star of Kismet. Mary Martin flew in that year in Peter Pan at the Winter Garden, and at Henry Miller's Theatre (now Xenon disco) Franchot Tone was starring in the hit Oh, Men! Oh Women!

Big movies lured the big crowds, too. Ray Milland was stalking Grace Kelly in Dial M for Murder

Continued on page 44

at the Paramount and hallucinating in Lost Weekend at the Rivoli. This Is Cinerama broke the record as the longest-running film on Broadway, and Marlon Brando was stunning audiences in On the Waterfront at the Astor. The Criterion featured Lew Ayres in Donovan's Brain, and at the Victoria a young Ronald Reagan was the star of Prisoner of War. You could see Eight Great Acts of Vaudeville at the Palace, but the films that went with them included such oddities as Donald O'Connor in Francis (the talking mule) Joins the WACS.

Other 1954 stars that made evenings in Times Square a treat were Judy Garland in A Star Is Born, John Wayne in The High and the Mighty, and Burt Lancaster in His Majesty O'Keefe, all of which opened at the Paramount. The Capitol was home to Jimmy Stewart in The Glenn Miller Story and Humphrey Bogart in The Caine Mutiny. Rock Hudson lured patrons to Loew's State with Magnificent Obsession; Loew's also held over Alan Ladd's Saskatchewan. At the Astor you could have seen Elizabeth Taylor in Elephant Walk or James Mason in 20,000 Leagues under the Sea. At the Criterion, the big hits were Grace Kelly's The Country Girl and Sabrina, in which Humphrey Bogart teamed up with Audrey Hepburn.

But in terms of showmanship, Times Square may never again see the likes of the night Robert Wagner showed up at a celebrity-studded 1954 premiere at the Roxy with a hairdo that would have put the Beatles to shame. But Wagner was entitled. He was the star of the film Prince Valiant. Its premiere, one of the first ever to be shown on television, was attended by such luminaries as the Duke of Windsor, William Randolph Hearst, and Laurence Rockefeller. It took place on the night of April 6, 1954, a few blocks north of the Crossroads of the World.

the hotel attained superstatus. After that, everybody who was anybody made it a point to be seen at the "great marble hotel." People like Mark Twain and General Grant had no complaints at all about the rates—a fireplace-equipped room rented for $2.50 a day —and that price included four sumptuous meals.

With the action shifted uptown, Delmonico's moved up too, first to 14th Street and then in 1876 to Fifth Avenue at 26th Street. Lorenzo Delmonico was no fool. It was estimated that there were 200 millionaires living on Fifth Avenue between 23rd and 42nd Streets in those days.

The foremost, of course, were Carrie Astor and her nephew, William Waldorf Astor, who lived next door to her at the corner of 33rd Street and Fifth. To say they didn't like each other would have been the understatement of the 1890s. Their feud came to a head in 1893 when young William built a 13-story hotel on the site of his mansion and ran off to England, chuckling about the "vulgar clamor" Aunt Carrie would have to put up with next door. The hotel was far from vulgar, but Mrs. Astor wasn't pleased. In 1897, she agreed to have an even more elegant hotel built on the site of her house. With the opening of Mrs. Astor's Waldorf-Astoria (not to mention her new mansion up on Fifth Avenue at 66th Street) the center of New York's night life took another giant step uptown.

In those days, no self-respecting hotel would be without a roof garden. The food there was a bit more expensive—the drinks were a lot more expensive—but nobody could refuse a chance to visit a roof garden, particularly at night. The Waldorf-Astoria's overlooked the lights of Fifth Avenue and cost the hotel $50,000 a year for flowers alone. But the garden that topped them all was the roof of the Astor Hotel, opened in 1905 by William Waldorf Astor at the corner of Broadway and 44th Street. At least 500,000 flowers were arranged among waterfalls and fountains. There were fish ponds and running streams, grottoes and gazebos dripping with baskets of ferns and honeysuckle, and an ivy-covered arbor that ran a full city block.

There was never a time in the history of the city that eating and drinking were done on such a grand scale as in the first two decades of the twentieth century. But at the stroke of midnight on January 15, 1920, it all came to an end: "The manufacture, sale or transportation of intoxicating liquor ... for beverage purposes is hereby prohibited," said the Constitution's Eighteenth Amendment. For the restaurants of the city it was a sentence of death. At the Plaza Hotel, the main dining room became an automobile showroom; a 42nd Street favorite known as Murray's Roman Garden became a flea circus.

While people in other cities found solace in reading great books or going to the movies during the '20s, New York entrepreneurs were busy inventing something they called "night clubs," designed to attract the many people who agreed with New York mayor Jimmy Walker that the greatest of all sins was going to bed the same day you got up. These clubs issued membership cards to attract a clientele, and many of the best ones could be found in what are New York's fancy neighborhoods today. The Maison Royale, on East 52nd Street just off Fifth Avenue, for example, is now the entrance to the public plaza in front of the posh Olympic Tower. The Park View Club and Jimmy's, both on Park Avenue, were torn down to make way for Lever House. The site of the Club Napoleon on East 56th Street is now occupied by the IBM building. When Prohibition was repealed, the owners of the Club Napoleon applied for a legitimate liquor license. They were turned down because their townhouse—with its deep carpets, tapestried walls, and marble fireplaces—had been too well-known as a speakeasy, and officials in Albany didn't like the reminder. The problem was simply solved with a name change to the Place Elegante.

Many of the buildings that housed those first night clubs are long gone. Some, like 38 East 52nd Street and 78 East 56th Street, have been replaced twice since the 1920s thanks to New York's penchant for tearing down and building new. But the beautiful Georgian building at 146–8 East 56th Street, site of the Merry-Go-Round, one of the most successful of the speaks, is still there. Another still intact and still operating under its original name is at 21 West 52nd Street, the fourth location of a successful speakeasy known as ''21.'' The wine cellars under the original brownstone still have secret panels for fast exits.

When the government lifted its siege at the end of 1933, a lot of speakeasies lifted their cover but still continued to call themselves night clubs. The Stork Club, which moved to 3 East 53rd Street (the site of the present-day Paley Park) in 1934 was among the most prosperous. El Morocco, on East 54th Street near Third Avenue, was among the first of the ''supper clubs'' and a favorite of the set who called themselves ''café society.'' The favorite of the Vanderbilts, and others who simply were Society, was the Colony, at Madison Avenue at 61st Street.

From post-repeal into the 1960s, New York night life boomed. There was something for everyone—from the Latin Quarter, upstairs at 48th Street between Broadway and Seventh Avenue, to Birdland, in a basement at Broadway and 52nd. You could get a great steak and listen to Louis Prima at the Hickory House on West 52nd Street or head over to Broadway and 51st Street and sample the cheesecake at Lindy's. Reuben's on East 58th Street off Fifth Avenue offered a ''celebrity sandwich,'' one remembered to this day as a Reuben sandwich.

To be sure, New York still has plenty of nighttime excitement —from discos where the management continues to follow the lead of the speakeasy operators, deciding on impulse who may or may not become a customer, to some of the best restaurants in the world. There may still be more prostitutes than there are Methodists, and there are indeed places tourists would be best advised to avoid. But when the sun goes down and the lights go on there is nothing in the world quite like New York. There never has been.

Back in 1968, Ann Reinking was a Radio City Music Hall Rockette. Then she met choreographer Bob Fosse, who put her in the chorus of the show Pippin'. *(He made her a full-fledged star in his 1978 Broadway hit* Dancin'.*) Armen Kachaturian recently discovered this moody portrait of her which he shot during the* Pippin' *days. (Armen Kachaturian)*

"No European city illuminated for a Coronation or a Jubilee could come near Broadway on a normal evening. It is a hundred Eiffel Towers, a thousand Rue Pigalle... luminous epilepsy, incandescent hypnotism. Pity the sky with nothing but stars."

—PHILIPPE DE ROTHSCHILD
PARIS, 1931

The Crown Building on 57th Street at Fifth Avenue was designed by the architects of Grand Central, Warren & Wetmore. (Mark Bauman)

The same architectural firm is also responsible for the Con Edison Building downtown on Irving Place at 14th Street. (Dudley Gray)

PREVIOUS PAGE
Floodlit buildings are such a familiar part of the Manhattan skyline, it's hard to believe they haven't always been illuminated. The Empire State Building was first with the idea in 1976. It's still one of the most dramatic and one of the few that works its charm from any angle, including the street below. (Chuck Dorris)

Warren & Wetmore designed this tower in the middle of Park Avenue at 46th Street as the headquarters of the New York Central Railroad. The name was changed to the New York General Building when the Central ceased to exist; it was an easy change for the stone carvers who had to alter the words over the door. It is now known as the Helmsley Building. (Marvin Newman)

ON THE FOLLOWING PAGES
There are 21,800 windows in the North Tower of the World Trade Center—300,000 square feet of glass. Most of the lights on each of the 110 one-acre floors are turned on and off by computer, so a lighted window doesn't necessarily mean someone is working inside. (Andy Levin/Black Star)

Most of the signs in Times Square these days are designs of flashing neon that advertise products made in Japan. The oldest of these neon spectaculars is the Coca-Cola sign at the north end of the Square, promoting a product as American as apple pie. (Ralf Manstein)

When the Brooklyn Bridge was built in 1883, its towers superceded the steeple of Trinity Church as the city's tallest structure. The bridge, with a main span of 1,595 feet, was also the longest suspension bridge in the world. Today 32 bridges, five of them in New York City, are longer. (Dan Lecca)

If you ask a native New Yorker to name a favorite skyscraper, the Chrysler Building is the most likely response. The white fluorescent lights in the crown were part of the original 1930 plan, but they weren't used for 50 years. It was worth the wait. The building looks sensational from every angle, even from Calvary Cemetery in Queens. (Kevin Moan)

When the Empire State Building celebrated its 50th anniversary in 1981, the occasion was marked with a laser light show from its tower. (Andy Levin/Black Star)

CITY STREETS

"Of course I drive at night! That medallion on the hood cost me fifty-five thousand bucks. I need to hustle. Bright lights? Listen, pal, the only lights I see are red ones and green ones. I see red, I stop; green, I go. You usually get the bigger tippers at night. They're out for a good time, see. Lots of guys tip big to impress the girl friend. I'm not complaining about that! I've got just one gripe... people who smoke in the cab. I'm allergic, you see."

—HARRY MORGENSTERN, CAB DRIVER
New York, 1983

St. Patrick's Cathedral on Fifth Avenue at 50th Street is floodlit in front from Rockefeller Center's International Building and in back from the top of the Helmsley Palace Hotel. (Howard Millard)

The Gem Spa on Third Avenue at St. Mark's Place is an active spot all night long. On Saturday nights, people from the East Village drop by for an early copy of the Sunday New York Times. (Don Hamerman)

There are over 30 major department stores headquartered in New York, and that adds up to a lot of window-shopping opportunities. Bergdorf Goodman's windows run for a full block on Fifth Avenue and spill over onto both 57th and 58th Streets. (Don Hamerman)

ON THE FOLLOWING PAGES
Except for special events, the Metropolitan Museum of Art is open only one night a week, Tuesday until 8:45. Even when it's closed, the museum's front steps are one of New York's best perches for seeing and being seen. (Mark Ivins)

What street compares with Mott Street? At night, even Broadway has a hard time competing. (James Nachtwey/Black Star)

Though more than 3 million people each year enjoy Central Park in the daytime, it's not a good idea to go for a walk there after dark. Still, the view of the skyline below 59th Street is most beautiful when viewed from the park at night. (Tom Zimberoff/Sygma)

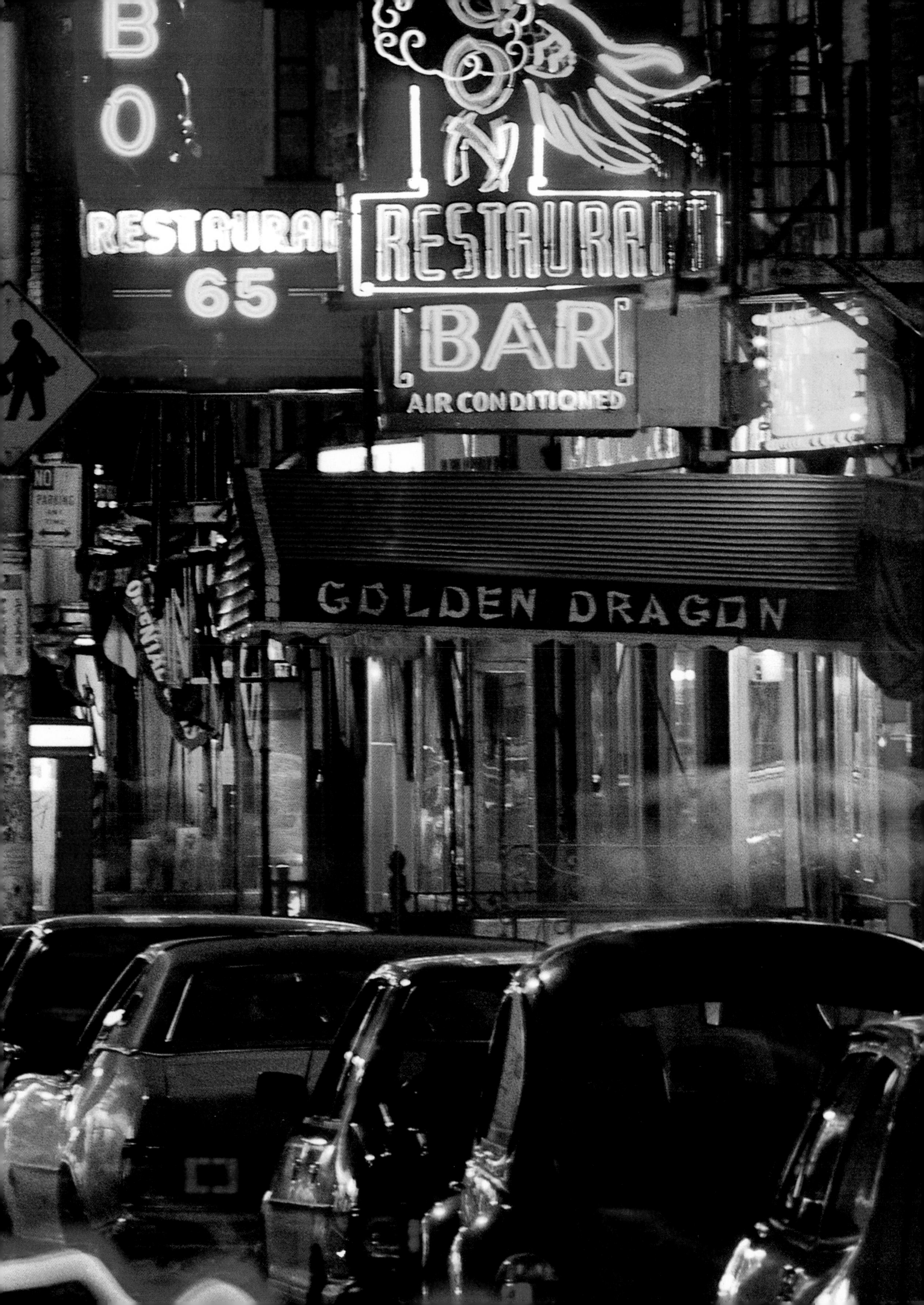
65
BAR
AIR CONDITIONED
GOLDEN DRAGON

B E N E A T H   T H E   S T R E E T S

"Everything is running just as smooth as oil. There is only one trouble for us that I can see. We are going to be bothered with sleepers. As we whizz along, the pillars come so fast that they give a frog-like effect to the folks looking out the windows. They half-close their eyes and the next thing you know they are sound asleep."

—MICHAEL J. HEANEY, SUBWAY GUARD
OPENING DAY, NEW YORK, 1904

There are 704.29 miles of subway track in New York—223.98 miles of it in Manhattan. One way to pass the time while waiting for a train at night is to watch the tunnel for the welcome twin headlights. (Both: Serge Hambourg)

N I G H T   S H I F T

"Night separates the world into two different kinds of people, those who are not bothered by uniforms and those who are threatened by them. One stops and chats, glad for the company; another tries to challenge what he feels is a symbol of authority. Like the guy who signed the register 'Richard Nixon.' But I like them all and I love this job. I'm a painter and I write poetry and I get plenty of time to think here at night. I love to watch the sun come up, first dimly and then casting a reddish glow over the buildings. That's when I get to go home and paint."

—Charles Roberts, Wall Street security guard
New York, 1983

Burning the midnight oil is a common occurrence among the captains of New York industry. How else can they keep ahead of the competition? (Don Hamerman)

Most of New York's great department stores, like Bonwit Teller, change their window displays at least once a week; but their daytime customers almost never see the work in progress. (Joe Vasta)

Street musicians find the parks to be their best territory during the day. But when the sun goes down, nothing beats Fifth Avenue, where there are window shoppers waiting to be serenaded. (Marianne Bernstein)

ON THE FOLLOWING PAGES
Many modern office buildings, hardly noticeable in the daytime, are a patchwork of light at night. This one on Park Avenue adds a festive note to the midtown skyline. (Jeff Perkell)

The entire country keeps in touch with New York at night thanks to programs like "NBC News Overnight," an institution that has helped make old movies old hat. (Don Hamerman)

A growing number of produce stands are open 24 hours a day in New York. One good reason is because it's easier to stay open than put all those mangoes and papayas away for the night. (Armen Kachaturian)

Owner Faith Stewart Gordon and her staff at the Russian Tea Room ("slightly to the left of Carnegie Hall") will treat you in a manner fit for a czar when you drop by after a concert some night. (Matthew Klein)

Someone once asked a New York restaurant critic to name his favorite restaurant: his answer was "Chinatown." With hundreds of restaurants and tea houses on the East Side below Canal Street, how can you go wrong? (Paul Elson)

D A N C I N G

"I'm here at Roseland every Thursday night from 6 o'clock until 10. I get paid $9.40 a night plus a dollar a dance. You thought it was a dime a dance, right? Well, that's inflation for you. We give them four minutes for a dollar these days. There are eleven women and six men working here, and we all do it because we just love it. Dancing is marvelous. It's better than Chinese food, which is better than sex. *That's* how much I love dancing!"

—SUSAN PETERS, TAXI DANCER
NEW YORK, 1982

The biggest dance floor in New York is the 10,000-square-foot floor at Roseland on West 52nd Street, where ballroom dancing is still a fine art. Disco begins after midnight on Saturdays. (Sonia Moskowitz)

Sometimes dancing can wear a person out. If it's a celebration at the Metropolitan Museum, the benches out front on Fifth Avenue are terrific for getting your second wind. (Marianne Bernstein)

As if the action isn't fast enough at the regular discos in town, they speed it up by adding wheels at the Roxy Roller Disco on West 18th Street. (John McGrail)

ON THE FOLLOWING PAGES
Back in the days when people were lining up to get into Studio 54, one reason was the spectacular entertainment provided to give the customers a chance to catch their breath. This trapeze artist was there to celebrate Valentine's Day. (Mariette Pathy Allen)

International visitors usually find their way to Regine's on Park Avenue. It has one of New York's best restaurants in front and a colorful disco in back. (Don Hamerman)

G R E A T P E R F O R M A N C E S

"The Big Apple at night is more than 'entertainment'—much more. When we New Yorkers go to the theater, the opera, or the dance, we're feeding our spirits. When we're sitting in Avery Fisher Hall, listening to the Philharmonic or leaning against the bar at Sweet Basil soaking up the jazz, we're taking in soul food through our ears. And we love sharing our experiences. Even if I'm at a play by myself, I know that someone will turn to me during intermission and ask, "Well, what do you think?" Or else, *I'll* pose the question. The only problem we New Yorkers have—and it's a big one—is that there's just too much ground to cover in one lifetime. That's why we all hope heaven is just like Broadway."

—Jack MacBean, vice president,
New York Convention & Visitors Bureau.

A beautiful place to hear beautiful music is the nearly acoustically perfect Carnegie Hall, which opened in 1891 with a concert by the New York Philharmonic conducted by Peter Ilich Tchaikovsky. (Carnegie Hall Photo)

Cats has the distinction of being the first show in the history of the Broadway theater to cost more than $5 million to produce. It also holds the record for advance ticket sales—$6.2 million before the first review appeared in September 1982. While 1,500 hopefuls were auditioning for the 30 parts in the show, orders were taken for 70,000 original cast albums. (Martha Swope)

ON THE FOLLOWING PAGES

The man in the moon is really Bosse Beite in a clever disguise devised for a performance by the British musical group Bloolips at the Orpheum Theater on Second Avenue at St. Mark's Place. (Jill Lynne)

The musical Little Shop of Horrors first opened Off Off Broadway at the WPA Workshop but was such a smash hit it reopened at the Orpheum, an Off Broadway theater. It's about a man who sells his soul to a man-eating cactus named Audrey. (Peter Cunningham)

The New York Philharmonic's home is Avery Fisher Hall in Lincoln Center, but in the summer the orchestra goes outdoors to give free concerts in the city's parks, including Central Park. (Scott Mlyn)

The New York Yankees play 81 games a season up in the Bronx at Yankee Stadium (and a few more if they get to the World Series). The stadium seats 56,000 fans, while millions more can catch the action on TV. (Don Hamerman)

A Christmas tradition that began long before the New York City Ballet moved to Lincoln Center's New York State Theater is its presentation of The Nutcracker. Everyone has a favorite scene; for many it's the promise of a white Christmas when it begins snowing on stage. (Steven Caras/The New York City Ballet)

C E L E B R A T I O N S

''The number of people who came down to see the fireworks was astonishing. From 6 :30 o'clock there was not an elevated train or surface car or stage coach that was not filled to suffocation.... At 8 o'clock precisely, Miss Laura C. Detwiller applied the torch to the first flight of 50 rockets. A grand line of fire shot up into the air and burst into a shower of golden rain and red, blue and emerald stars.... Fourteen tons of fireworks were burned on the Brooklyn Bridge last night.''

—THE *New York Times*
NEW YORK, MAY 25, 1883

New York may be the only city in the world whose bureaucracy includes a "fireworks commissioner." George Plimpton is the first and only person to hold this honorary title, and he presided over this typical Fourth of July spectacular. (David Moore)

The Christmas season officially begins when Macy's stages its Thanksgiving Day Parade. The best part is watching Underdog and the other giant balloons getting high on helium at the edge of Central Park in the wee hours of the morning. (Mariette Pathy Allen)

ON THE FOLLOWING PAGES
In 1931, workers digging the hole that would become the Rockefeller Center skating rink put up a 12-foot Christmas tree on the construction site. The following year, the Rockefellers put up their own 65-foot tree in the newly created plaza, and they've been doing it ever since. The 1982 tree was a 70-foot Norway spruce that grew in Mahwah, New Jersey. Its 35-foot branches were decorated with 10,000 colored lights, which were thrown away when the tree was taken down. The tree itself was ground up for mulch. (Left: Andy Levin/Black Star; right: Hiroyuki Matsumoto/Black Star)

"If you haven't seen Macy's, you haven't seen New York," they say. If you haven't seen its Broadway entrance decorated for Christmas, where do you get your Christmas spirit? (Hiroyuki Matsumoto/Black Star)

Halloween is the one dark night of the year when meeting the Grim Reaper could be a pleasant experience. (Viviane Holbrooke)

For many, the best of all New York nights is Halloween, when all types of fantasy can be indulged. The parade winds through the streets of Greenwich Village and should not be missed. (All: Marvin Newman)

OVERLEAF
Just taking the dogs for a walk can be an adventure. (Mariette Pathy Allen)

D I N I N G   O U T

''Diversity is the city's specialty.... And because it has the country's most demanding audience, many chefs and restaurant owners say they feel challenged to test their mettle here. If New York does not rival Paris, Tokyo, or such northern Italian cities as Milan, Venice, and Florence as a source of trend-setting culinary innovation, it makes up for that by offering a far wider selection of ethnic cuisines of remarkably high quality.''

—MIMI SHERATON, RESTAURANT CRITIC OF THE *New York Times*
NEW YORK, 1983

Ask New York Mayor Ed Koch for the name of his favorite restaurant and he probably won't tell. It's one of his little secrets. Playing favorites has never been good politics. (Paul Elson)

On a Broadway opening night, the place the stars and their producers gather after the show to await the news from the critics is Sardi's on West 44th Street. (Don Hamerman)

Maxwell's Plum on Second Ave. It's been imitated a thousand times, but nothing quite matches the original. (Armen Kachaturian)

ON THE FOLLOWING PAGES

The budget for flowers at La Grenouille on East 52nd Street runs as high as $75,000 a year. That's just one reason why fashionable New Yorkers consider it one of the best restaurants in town. The food is legendary. (Armen Kachaturian)

A favorite with young people, McSorley's Old Ale House on East 7th Street claims to be the oldest drinking establishment in the city. In the 1960s the National Organization for Women turned this "for men only" establishment into a place open to everyone. When NOW demonstrators first showed up they were welcomed with a shower of ale. (Don Hamerman)

The Beautiful People choose the Art Deco Empire Diner for late-night snacks. It's been among the "in" places longer than most, possibly because it has been at the same Tenth Avenue location for longer than many of its customers have been alive. (Hugues Colson)

The Crystal Room at Tavern on the Green in Central Park at West 67th Street has a collection of chandeliers that includes one that was used in the film Gone with the Wind. (Armen Kachaturian)

There are 578 miles of waterfront in New York City, but very few restaurants overlook the water. The Water Club on the East River at the end of 30th Street does, and it's one of the best places in town to wait for the sunrise. (Don Hamerman)

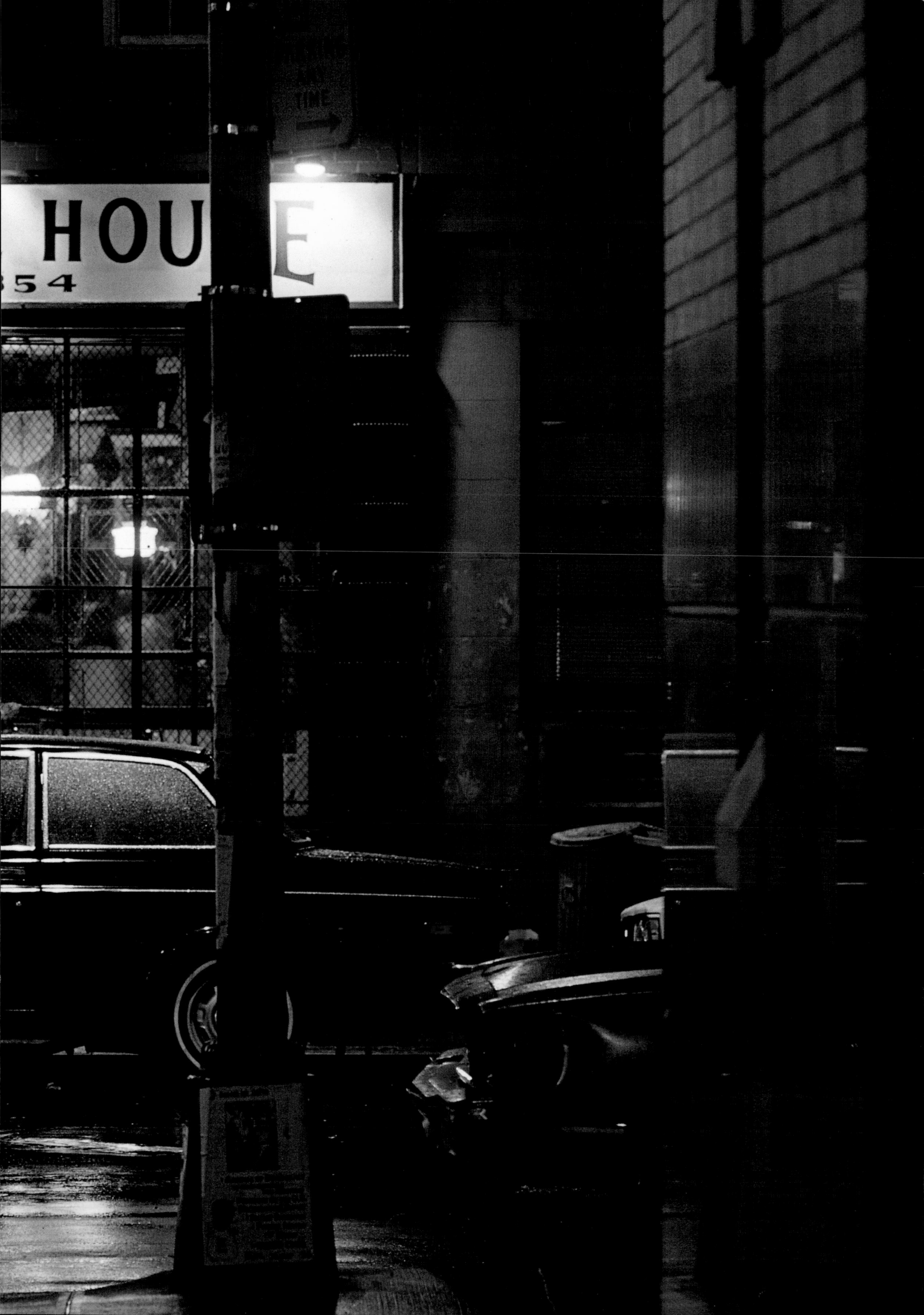
HOU E
354

IN NEW YORK, NIGHT BECOMES OFFICIAL WHEN AN ELEC-
tric timer turns on the 204 floodlights that illuminate the Empire
State Building above its 71st floor. Seconds later, 310 fluorescent
lamps in the mooring mast tower blink on, and life in the city
takes on a whole new aspect.

In the streets a peculiar phenomenon is taking place as the
day ends—a phenomenon that New Yorkers, world famous for
their ironic sense of humor, refer to as the "rush hour." No one
knows for sure how many cars, trucks, and buses are on their
way into or out of Manhattan on any given evening between
5:00 and 7:00; but if any of these drivers are in a rush they've
picked the wrong time.

A great many commuters have found a solution to the problem,
however. It begins well before the evening rush and often continues well beyond it. It's what accommodating bar owners call
"happy hour." Happiness comes in the form of reduced prices
in many places, free snacks in others. Either way, "happy hour"
regulars agree it's a terrific way to beat crowded trains and buses
and to avoid traffic jams.

Many Manhattanites tend to sidestep the crowded trains of
rush hour by putting on their running shoes and walking or jog-
ging home from work. In fact, many even consider this the ideal
time to get in their exercise—rather than waiting to get home
and change. The sight of Adidas sneakers with three-piece suits
or daytime dresses has become so common on the sidewalks of
New York that people hardly notice anymore.

If the walkers happen to live in the Gramercy Park area and
their route takes them past the corner of Third Avenue and 23rd
Street, chances are they'll notice a pretty young woman stand-
ing in front of a cigar store and holding a microphone in her
hand. At precisely 6:00 every weekday evening, she faces a TV
camera and begins speaking in Japanese. Her image is picked
up by a satellite for transmission to Los Angeles. It goes from
there by land lines to San Francisco and then to another satellite
to be bounced to Tokyo where she appears "live" on the Tokyo
Broadcasting System in a show millions know and love as "Asa
No Hot-Line."

The English translation, in case you didn't know, is "Morning
Hot-Line." When it's 6:00 tonight at 23rd and Third, it's 7:00
tomorrow morning in neighborhoods like Shinjuku and Ikeburo.
The woman on the Manhattan street corner is either Shirley Masuo
or Judith Anton, one of the sisters who write and star in the "Hot-
Line" show, a five-minute daily presentation of what's going on
in New York.

Most evenings about 6:00 the street corner that provides the
show's setting is among the busiest in town. It's within a block of
both the School of Visual Arts and City University's Bernard Baruch
College. Both schools are as active in the evening as they are
during the day, and this is an hour of changing classes.

*If you think the Sunday New York
Times is too heavy to carry home,
consider this: each of these heavy
rolls of newsprint weighs 1,700
pounds, and 650 of them are delivered every day to the Times
Building on West 43rd Street. The
average Sunday edition uses 3,000
tons of paper. (Don Hamerman)*

*They stopped showing movies at
Radio City Music Hall in 1979,
but people still line up around the
block to see the Christmas show.
(Jim Smith)*

OVERLEAF TOP
*Grand Central Terminal's main
waiting room is one of the biggest
enclosed spaces in the world and
has been called "the crossroads of
a million lives." No one crosses its
marble floor after 1:30 in the
morning, though; the station is
closed for the night at that hour.
(Michael Soluri)*

OVERLEAF BOTTOM
*On the other hand, over on Broad-
way at 42nd Street, "the Crossroads of the World," the corner
newsstand is open all night long—
as are 35 others in Manhattan.
(Michael Soluri)*

Just about all the 89 colleges and universities in the city offer evening classes, and more than 30 percent of their total enrollment is people who work all day and go to school at night, probably after dining on a Sabrette frankfurter and a Coke from one of the streetcorner wagons whose umbrellas add a bright touch to the midtown scene. It can take up to 15 years to get a law degree this way, but for some New Yorkers it is the only way. An even greater percentage of nighttime students are enrolled in what the colleges like to call "job skill and self-help" courses, where they learn such things as how to communicate with a computer or how to out-fox their bosses.

Some courses, with titles like "The Films of Fellini" or "How to Buy a Co-op Apartment," often seem to attract participants more interested in meeting each other. One evening course, "Meeting People at the Great Museums," is even advertised as a "hands on" experience: for $45 plus a $5 registration fee an art historian explains enough about the paintings along Fifth Avenue's Museum Mile for any student to be able to strike up an intelligent conversation there on a Sunday afternoon. Of course, not all of New York's evening education occurs in traditional environments, and teaching is not always done by professional educators. A woman on the Upper East Side offers courses in Afghan cooking in her apartment; another will teach you how to knit an afghan in her SoHo loft.

Talk about learning to Harry Freudenheim and he'll tell you about night people he's met time and again who never seem to learn a thing. Harry is a police officer who works out of the Midtown South precinct on West 35th Street. He spends a lot of evening hours at the Manhattan Night Arraignment Court, downtown in the Criminal Courts Building at 100 Centre Street. "Some of these characters are here two, three times a month," says Harry. "If you believe the things they tell the judge, they never seem to know why we brought them here."

Night court convenes at 6:00 P.M. and handles a steady stream of cases until 1:00 A.M. In an average year about a quarter of the defendants who appear there are charged with felonies—the most serious category of criminal charge. The only busier court in the city is the night court on Schermerhorn Street in Brooklyn; here, on a typical night, a judge may dispose of a case every two minutes, and the rate of felony charges often runs as high as 40 percent of the caseload.

The purpose of having courts in session in the evening is to give defendants a chance to have the charges against them dismissed or to have bail set so they might avoid spending the night in jail waiting for the more formal courts to open in the morning. Prostitutes and petty thieves, drug dealers and boisterous drunks who have been charged with disturbing the peace mingle with police officers in civilian clothes, identifiable only by the badges dangling from their belts, and with Legal Aid lawyers and representatives of the District Attorney's office.

Behind the scenes at Dreamgirls *—the musical loosely based on the career of the* Supremes—*at the Imperial Theater. (All: Don Hamerman)*

Some nights it's tough to tell the good guys from the bad guys, but it's always easy to figure out who's just visiting night court. Spectators are discreetly separated from the perpetrators and the representatives of the criminal justice system by a length of chain. The people behind it are often New Yorkers looking for something a little different in the way of entertainment. "I usually bring dates here," explains Sam Eisenberg, a Columbia University student. "It's free, for one thing, and it always gives the girls something to tell their friends about."

There is room for about 150 people at a time to watch this free real-life drama down on Centre Street. Uptown in the Theater District there are seats for more than 46,000 people in 42 theaters. But theater is far from free. Prices run as high as $50 apiece. Curtain time for most shows is 8:00 and, according to Catherine Bliven, who has been an usher in a variety of New York theaters for more than 30 years, the majority of theatergoers never seem to arrive until 7:59.

Miss Bliven is one of 300 women dressed in black pantsuits with white lace collars who lead theater patrons to the right seats, press *Playbills* into their hands, and field minor complaints. The ushers arrive for work at 7:00 and they're kept busy until about 8:15, at which time they're free until intermission.

Today, most of Miss Bliven's co-workers are young women who are more apt to be aspiring actresses than career ushers. The pay for their 20-hour work week doesn't amount to much more than the cost of a pair of orchestra seats for the average musical, but it gets them into an environment they can't resist, and many are quick to point out that it beats waiting on tables.

It does, that is, if the young actress happens to be independently wealthy. Many who work as ushers are forced to take second jobs to keep body and soul together, leaving them less time to audition. That gives a slight edge to other theater hopefuls who work at serving pre-theater dinners and post-theater suppers in restaurants all over the Times Square area.

When the theatergoers are finally in their seats, the smart New Yorkers go out for dinner. "Dinner at eight" has been a New York tradition for a long time, and New Yorkers know that a fine meal, well presented, is an adventure in itself. Eating out is the one thing most of them get passionate about. And, with the possible exception of the weather, the Number One topic of conversation around the city is exchanging information about new restaurants or treasured old favorites. For some people "dinner at eight" is a relaxing end to the evening; for others it is an exciting prelude to the night ahead.

IT IS ESTIMATED THAT, IN MANHATTAN ALONE, 200,000 MEN and women work all night—more people than live in a city the size of Syracuse, New York. A large percentage of people who regularly work at night often find their lives twisted around, and many agree with Benjamin Franklin that "early to bed and early

The greatest fights of the century, they say, have been fought in New York, especially in Madison Square Garden. The tradition continues. (James Hamilton)

OVERLEAF
Joan Sutherland and Luciano Pavarotti enthusiastically accept the applause of the audience at a Lincoln Center gala. (Scott Mlyn)

to rise" probably is the best way to stay healthy, wealthy, and wise. A government study of people whose work requires them to go to bed early in the morning and get up in mid-afternoon has shown that apparently Ben was right about the healthy part. The study found that people on the night shift suffer more cramps, colds, and chest pains than people on the nine-to-five shift. They drink more; they're inclined to wheeze a lot; and they seem more prone to stomach problems.

If you believe Barbara Rosenberg, a night nurse at the New York Hospital–Cornell Medical Center, night workers might also be a bit overweight. "I find it hard to eat a real meal on this schedule," she says, "and so I live on cakes and cookies. I've gained so much weight on this job you wouldn't believe it!" The schedule hasn't been too terrific for her social life, either. "I feel left out a lot of the time," she admits. "It's like I'm missing something."

But would Barbara trade places with the woman who replaces her in the morning? Don't bet on it! She likes going to and from work against the flow of rush-hour traffic. She loves shopping when the stores first open, before the saleshelp gets cranky and while the merchandise is still neat and orderly. In summer she likes being able to go to the beach on weekdays, and in winter the sun keeps her apartment cozy and warm during the hours she's home.

Similarly, before he retired in 1960, after 35 years as drama critic of the *New York Times*, Brooks Atkinson made the appeal of working at night perfectly clear: "Don't waste sympathy on the people who work at night," he wrote. "Don't pity us. We pity you. The act of going solemnly to work while other people are sitting at home in their slippers, gaping at television, playing cards or possibly carousing, induces a feeling of puritanical piety, as though we're the only responsible people in the world."

Each night at about 9:45 copies of the first edition of tomorrow's *New York Times* are already being delivered to newsstands around the city, while each of nine presses continuously spew out ten copies a second, folded and ready for sale throughout the world. The copies of *The Times* earmarked for mail subscribers are wrapped in brown paper, labeled, and delivered to the General Post Office at Eighth Avenue and 33rd Street, adding 18,000 pieces of mail to the total of 4,000,000 this Post Office estimates it handles each day of the year. The bundles get to the busiest post office building in the world at precisely its busiest hour. The place may be a wasteland at 3:00 in the afternoon, but by 10:00 in the evening it's a madhouse—of hand trucks, conveyor belts, cancelling machines, and hundreds of workers rushing to process 45,000 pieces of mail each hour. The same scene is repeated in two more of the 59 branches the Postal Service operates in Manhattan: the Morgan on Ninth Avenue and the Church Street Station. But of these three, the Eighth Avenue

New York firefighters are as much in the business of saving lives as of fighting fires. (The New York Daily News)

The firefighters' gear is as ready as they are for any emergency that comes to Engine Company 9. (Don Hamerman)

building is the only one where you can buy a stamp in the middle of the night, 365 days a year.

The night is just as busy down in the financial district, where computers have turned Wall Street into a 24-hour operation. It used to be that people who worked all night in downtown banks and brokerage houses, processing the transactions that took place during the day, were assigned to special office areas apart from the large spaces used by their daytime counterparts. Fewer people were needed then than during the day, and it was felt that people working in small groups in large spaces suffered symptoms of loneliness that slowed productivity. Furthermore, landlords charged huge fees to keep the bigger spaces cooled in the summer and heated in winter. Few companies found the extra expense worthwhile—until they began installing computers.

Once machines completely replaced the little men in green eyeshades, companies were forced to accommodate them with a temperature-controlled environment, and it made sense to get more out of the investment by keeping the computers operating 24 hours a day. That meant that the people who watched over them had to be on hand all night long. It was a movement that changed the character of The Street.

In the mid-1960s, the newsstand tucked into a corner of the New York Stock Exchange Building at Broad and Wall Streets closed every evening at 7:00 and some nights even earlier. By 1970, it was open all night and doing a thriving business. A few blocks away, down on Broad Street, the Deli-O Sandwich & Hero Shop, which used to open at 6 A.M., now begins its business day at 1:00 in the morning. Several years ago the owners began to notice that there wasn't time to set up for breakfast because of the long line of hungry customers waiting outside when they got there. The owners tried arriving at 5:30, but people were still banging on the windows. They finally faced reality and, by opening at 1:00, got the benefits of an extra "lunch hour" each day.

The increase in the number of night workers in New York's financial community has brought another traditional daytime worker into the ranks of New York's night people: the bank officer. Until recently, many night workers considered themselves forgotten people. To be sure, many liked the idea of not having the Big Boss watching over their shoulders, but once corporate VPs started joining them they admitted to feeling more important to the organization. Still, the executives won't make a career of the night shift. By policy, most banks don't require their officers to serve on that shift for more than a year or so. And as one young Citibank vice president on the twelve-to-eight shift explains it, "I expect to be noticed."

Of course, not everyone considers the night shift a necessary rung on the corporate ladder. Sam Kellerman, who has worked nights for a big stock brokerage firm since he began his working life in the mid-1950s, says, "It starts to get busy here at about 9

If you're an old-fashioned guy who thinks real men don't go to beauty parlors—but you're curious about the experience—you can go under cover of darkness to Heads & Tales on St. Mark's Place. (Don Hamerman)

P.M. That's when the Hong Kong Exchange opens up. Tel Aviv comes on at about 2:00, and after that we just follow the sun: Munich, Geneva, Paris, London. I'm long gone by the time it reaches New York. And that's the way I like it."

With all that night work going on in Manhattan office towers, keeping them clean can be a problem. Computer complexes are constantly being cleaned because the machines require a dust-free as well as cool environment, and the people who work there have to get used to lifting their feet when the sweeper comes around. But by and large, office buildings in New York are tidied up as if this were still a nine-to-five town.

At exactly 5:45 every weekday evening, for instance, 115 cleaning women in neat green uniforms fan out to preassigned locations in the Empire State Building. By midnight, they will have made 2,176,422 square feet of offices neat as a pin. In those same hours, down in the twin towers of the World Trade Center, the cleaning staff and many late workers are racing against the clock. Each of the 107 tenant floors in each tower is divided into four sections, and the lights in most quarters are plugged into a computer. At a predetermined time—different for each section, depending on the needs of the tenant—the computer pulls the plug. Once the lights go out, there is no way to turn them back on again until electronic wizardry lights up the offices at about 7:30 in the morning. Many cleaning people in the twin towers carry flashlights—just in case.

The lights never go out in New York's fire houses, police stations, and hospital emergency rooms, where the people working the post-midnight shift spend a lot of time waiting for something to happen. These people do just what you'd expect them to do. They play games. What sort of games? Chess seems to be the hands-down winner, and there are hundreds of chess games going on all over town in the middle of the night. It's probably because the game can be interrupted and reconstructed hours—or even days—later. And chess keeps minds alert. It also doesn't lead to gambling, which could have a negative effect on the extra pay nightworkers collect for having their lives turned around.

Possibly the most dedicated late-night chess players may be found among the people who staff the approximately 100 ambulances that the city's Emergency Medical Service has on the streets during the night. Though each team works in a specific part of the city, it's not uncommon for an EMS ambulance to deliver patients to two or three different hospitals on a single tour of duty, and it's a good bet they have a chess game going at each hospital.

Though Bob Dunn has an assistant to help see him through the night, he spends most of his off time watching television. Bob is a tugboat dispatcher who says he never took up chess because his job is too much like the game. He keeps track of every move every McAllister tug makes all night long. The crews he watches and dispatches to new assignments not only work

At night you can usually get a seat on the subway if you want one. But sometimes there are more important things to do than sit around. (Sylvia Plachy)

through the night, they work 72-hour shifts, sleeping and eating on board between jobs. If Bob sends them around to pick up a ship at Elizabeth, New Jersey, at 3:00 A. M., it's all in a day's work to them.

Meanwhile, on shore, 3:00 in the morning is still the shank of the evening for a lot of people. Musicians, bartenders, cab drivers, and hoteliers are among those dedicated to making sure their customers know that New York at night is where the good times are even though the clock says three. While most other U.S. cities have long since closed down for the night, in New York the action never stops.

IT'S 3:30 IN THE MORNING AT THE CORNER OF 59TH STREET and Fifth Avenue. The Plaza Hotel's room service is delivering two rare steaks and a bottle of champagne to the guests in Room 802. In the next 15 minutes, room service will answer six more calls from other hungry guests.

Meanwhile, downstairs in the Plaza's Oak Room restaurant, the small army of sixty people at work filming a movie decide they too are hungry and declare this to be their lunch hour. As is the case with all film crews working on location, the unions require that the producer feed them on the job. Nothing in their contract requires him to provide sixty Oak Room dinners though, and to save money, this producer has hired a caterer. But the contract between the Plaza and the union that represents its food and beverage people forbids outside caterers to use the hotel's facilities. The caterer solves this by setting up tables on the sidewalk outside facing Central Park, and in the next 15 minutes, the Plaza is graced by what amounts to a sidewalk café. At 3:30 in the morning.

As the film people line up for "lunch," a group of German tourists is lining up across the street to be photographed with a llama named Chiqui. The llama is in the neighborhood most nights at this hour, usually delivered by a Checker cab on his way home from a party, having been rented out as the star attraction by his owner, Martin Munoz, a painter and poet by day. Munoz is the native South American of the pair; Chiqui comes from Massachusetts.

Close by, four of the city's fleet of 68 horse-drawn carriages are still on the job. Between 3:30 and 3:45, two of them are hired by the German tourists, one for a ride through Central Park, the other for a trip down Fifth Avenue and back up Madison.

Four other people on the corner of 59th and Fifth have chosen a more modern means of transportation downtown. At 3:55, right on schedule, an M1 bus picks them up for a trip toward Greenwich Village. The bus is already carrying 20 people, including a group of interns from Mount Sinai Hospital and young Arnie Eagan, a Columbia University student who is on his way for a date with his friend Amanda, a waitress in a Bleeker Street jazz club. His plan is to pick up Amanda when the club closes, then to shop for records at Bleeker Bob's Golden Oldies.

Eye contact on the subway is usually something to be avoided. But sometimes you can't resist. (Jim Smith)

In 1982, the number of felonies in the subway dropped for the first time in seven years, thanks, in part, to special nighttime police patrols. (Jim Smith)

Subway artists aren't shy about signing their work, but it's rare to see one at work. (Jim Smith)

Amanda will need the relaxation. Twenty minutes before closing she suddenly has her hands full with a group of teenagers from Long Island who have had a bit too much to drink. One of them is determined that before the night ends he is going to have a marijuana leaf tattooed to his forearm. Not all his friends agree it's a good idea, and the argument is loud. Amanda suggests they take their discussion out into the street where they might also find a tattoo artist. What none of them knows is that the city of New York settled the argument back in 1961 by making tattooing illegal anywhere in the five boroughs.

But if you can't get tattooed at 3:40 in the morning, you can go bowling at the Bowlmor lanes on University Place or play Space Invaders at Playland on Broadway at 48th Street. You might even grab a cab to Queens and get in a few sets of tennis at the Alley Pond Indoor Tennis Courts. If your idea of fun is more cerebral, you can pick up a copy of the New York Times at any one of 36 locations in Manhattan and do the puzzle.

Unless you know a hairdresser who moonlights, you can't get a shampoo and set at 3:30 A.M., in spite of the fact that there is a place on Madison Avenue that calls itself The 24-hour Beauty Salon (it never stays open past 10:00 in the evening). But you can have the kink taken out of your back by Dr. B. P. Sheryll, an all-night chiropractor on West 57th Street. What, no kink? Every disco in town is open until 4:00 A.M., and a half-dozen are open later than that.

When Arnie Eagan finally gets to the jazz club, he discovers that more customers than usual have responded to Amanda's last call for drinks, and she'll have to stay on the job until they've finished. Since it's a nice night, Arnie decides to go for a stroll.

A lot of people might tell you that anyone who would go out for a walk anywhere in the middle of Manhattan in the middle of the night is either a drunk, an out-of-towner, or a fool. Arnie Eagan is none of those. But here in Greenwich Village at 4:00 in the morning he has no doubts that he will live to tell the tale.

There are 6,200 miles of streets in the five boroughs of New York City. Protecting the 26 or so miles that wander through Greenwich Village is the responsibility of the 160 police officers assigned to the 6th Precinct, which boasts one of the lowest rates of street crime in the city.

As usual, on this particular night the night shift went out at 11:45 P.M.. But recent budget cuts have reduced the number of patrolmen on duty to the unusual low of six. Between 3:30 and 3:45 A.M., two of them are called upon to defuse a domestic argument. Fortunately, by the time the patrol car gets over to Christopher Street to deal with this difference of opinion, the argument has cooled somewhat. The solution, the couple has decided, is for one of them to move out.

But Howard doesn't want to move out next month or next week or even tomorrow. He wants to move out right now. Fortunately, this is New York where anything is possible, even moving all

In police parlance, an arrest is a "collar." In this instance, the perpetrator's sleeve is more significant. Those dark stains are blood. (Don Hamerman)

your belongings at 3:45 in the morning. In fact, before the police arrive on the scene, Howard has called Kathy Kelley, a private mover who specializes in such things, and she is already driving her truck down Second Avenue to pick up her crew. The move will be accomplished well before dawn. Everyone knew it would. This is the sixth time in as many months Kathy has moved Howard to his mother's in the middle of the night.

Between 3:30 and 3:35, ten cars pull in for the night at the Perry Abingdon Garage not far away; Sky Way Plumbing on Seventh Street responds to an emergency call from a brownstone owner with an overactive fire sprinkler; and the A-Art Discount Locksmiths sends specialists out from their base at Second Avenue and 12th Street to help two different people who have lost the keys to their apartments.

At about the same time, Harriet Leonard, who runs a ceramics school on Columbus Avenue, is returning to her studio after a late-night consultation with her numerologist. The two of them have worked out a scheme to beat the New York State Lottery. It requires that Harriet buy 12 tickets and she can't wait.

Unfortunately, she'll have to wait. Knowledgeable lottery players know it's best to buy their tickets at stores equipped with computer terminals; this guarantees that their selections are properly recorded. But the only terminal-equipped store in Manhattan open all night is the Talk of the Town cigar store on the northwest corner of 42nd Street and Seventh Avenue. Even if Harriet had the foolish courage to invade Times Square at 4:00 in the morning, she'd find that the central computer the terminal is linked to shuts down at 11:00 every evening.

But Harriet already knew that. She's had this sort of late-night inspiration before. It's the first time she's consulted with a numerologist, though. Now she's so certain she'll be a millionaire in a few days that this chronic insomniac will be in bed by 3:45, sleeping like a baby, having counted dollar signs instead of sheep.

A half-dozen other New Yorkers have also just settled down to sleep. They are passengers aboard Amtrak's Night Owl, which arrived at Penn Station from Boston at 3:03 and pulled out bound for Washington D. C. at 3:33. They sleep secure knowing that they will be in the capital in time for breakfast meetings at 8:00.

This train is just about the only public transportation out of New York after 3:00 in the morning. There are no scheduled passenger flights from LaGuardia, Kennedy, or Newark Airports between 3:10 and 5:45 A.M. The 20 buses that go in and out of the Port Authority Bus Terminal in the wee hours generally go no further than the New Jersey suburbs. And after trains leave for North White Plains and for Stamford at 1:30 A.M., the Metropolitan Transportation Authority closes Grand Central Terminal completely until the commuters begin pouring back into New York in the morning. So if you're too late for public transportation and you need to leave the city, your best option is to rent a car from Avis on East 43rd Street.

A booking and a drug bust enliven the 6th Precinct in Greenwich Village, normally the quietest station house in the city. (Both: Don Hamerman)

Though the trains to Connecticut and Westchester don't run all night, the New York subway system does. There aren't many places in the world where any form of public transport operates around the clock, and in New York late-night subway riders are often treated to sights daytime commuters never see. Every night, gangs of men in orange reflector vests roam the system's 704 miles of track, taking sections apart and hurrying to get them put back together again before the morning rush begins. The late-night hours are also the best time to clean out the candy wrappers and copies of yesterday's newspaper that have accumulated on the tracks and in the stations. Six special trash trains haul the stuff out every night, and by morning four tons of passenger-generated debris are waiting in the yards to be hauled away by city sanitation trucks.

Four tons is just a drop in the bucket as far as the Sanitation Department is concerned, though. They pick up 15,000 tons of trash every single day even though they aren't the only garbage collection game in town. What they don't pick up is gathered by the 2,000 people who work for the private sanitation companies that serve restaurants, hotels, and other businesses. They go to work in earnest between 3:30 and 3:45 in the morning because many of the bars and restaurants that hire them don't close until 4:00 and they try to time their arrivals to avoid disturbing the patrons.

Some of these patrons, of course, may only be just starting their night on the town, and peace and quiet is the last thing they're looking for. It shouldn't be a problem. According to the New York Convention and Visitors Bureau, there are 30 night clubs in the city and another 60 classified as "night spots." The distinction here is that the "night spots" provide entertainment but not dancing. The bureau hasn't bothered to count discos, possibly because the number varies almost from night to night. The night crowd is a fickle one, and today's "in" spot can easily become tomorrow's Siberia. To prevent it from happening to them, owners often provide free drinks, drugs, or anything else that seems to be required by television actors, rock stars, and the so-called glitterati who seem interesting enough to attract paying customers.

But the beautiful people are only one aspect of the action at 3:30 A.M. Out at LaGuardia Airport's Marine Terminal, for instance, 3:30 is the average arrival time for a small private plane making a night run from Pittsburgh. Its cargo is hundreds of checks often totaling as much as $130,000. The checks are drawn on New York banks, and it's worth the expense of the plane to get the money quickly cleared and credited back to Pittsburgh where the bankers out there think it belongs. At the main terminal the plane is met by a helicopter, and its cargo is transferred and rushed off to the Wall Street Heliport (open at night for paying customers). Here a bank messenger picks it up and delivers it to a small building across from Fraunces Tavern on Broad Street.

The Animal Medical Center on East 62nd Street is often busier at night than during the day. If you find a stray in the middle of the night, you can bring it here for a check-up.   (All: Don Hamerman)

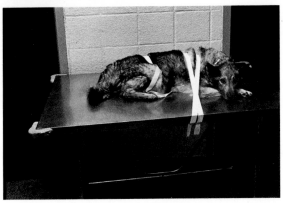

These checks are but a small part of the $18 billion worth of uncollected checks and drafts that go through the New York Clearing House each night. Under Clearing House rules, its member banks, including six of the biggest in the country, are required to pick up the checks credited to their accounts promptly at 10:00 in the morning. If they don't arrive in time, the Clearing House assesses a $5 fine, about half what some member banks charge their customers for a single rubber check. The fine is what passes for wit on Wall Street. But what is important is the cash flow. A check not processed by the 10:00 A.M. deadline waits until the following morning, which is why the Pittsburgh bank and others like it dispatch private airplanes to New York in the middle of the night.

About the same time the helicopter sets down on the East River pier that has been converted into a heliport, *The McAllister Brothers*, one of about 75 tugboats operating in the harbor at that hour, is assisting a containership downriver from a pier just north of the Manhattan Bridge. On the FDR Drive, a taxicab belonging to the Ding-A-Ling fleet is taking a fare uptown, after having answered a radio call to the Staten Island Ferry. As he cruises up the highway, the driver hears two other calls on his radio, both pickups from midtown bars with fares going to Queens and Brooklyn. Across the river in Brooklyn, Con Edison's Hudson Avenue Power plant, one of eight in the city but the only one in Brooklyn, is generating its share of the 3000 megawatts of electrical power usually required at this hour. The load is equal to peak output in many cities, but is only about half of New York's daytime requirement.

Back downtown, just off the tip of Manhattan on Governor's Island, two senior Coast Guard officers and 26 enlisted men are monitoring the activities in the port. They are using a variety of devices ranging from radar to radio telephones and even including a regular telephone hotline for the public to use to report oil spills. In these early hours of the morning and on until dawn, marine traffic in and out of the harbor is as heavy as in the daytime; ships pass in and out at over one an hour.

At 3:35, the H&H Bagel Bakery on Broadway and 80th is taking six dozen pumpernickel bagels from the oven while another six dozen, destined to be poppy-seeded, are coming out of the boiling water, ready for baking. Across town, a chartered bus is moving into Queens through the Queens-Midtown Tunnel. Only one passenger is aboard. It is Louise McAllen, a licensed New York City tour guide on her way to Kennedy Airport to start sorting out luggage belonging to a group of tourists who will arrive from Rio de Janiero on a Varig flight due in at 6:30.

Although there are no passenger planes coming or going from Kennedy at 3:30 in the morning, the place is lit bright as midday. Several hundred people are on the job, moving freight from the underbellies of cargo jets onto waiting trucks or into warehouses to wait for custom brokers who will sort it all out in the morning.

It's sometimes hard to remember that Times Square got its name when the New York Times *moved there in 1904. Prior to that it was known as Longacre Square. The* Times *does its best to remind you, though, with its fleet of trucks that deliver the papers, printed in the basement of its 43rd Street building. (Don Hamerman)*

Passengers aboard the Staten Island ferry at 3:00 A.M. take advantage of the empty benches to catch a little shut-eye. (Don Hamerman)

The Staten Island ferry's crew includes a sea-going porter and a conductor, both working the all-night shift. (Don Hamerman)

Post midnight clean-up at WQXR.
(Don Hamerman)

For more than 15 years Barry Farber's interview program on WMCA radio has been bringing the issues to late-night listeners. (Don Hamerman)

Before it's "Today" at NBC-TV, it's tonight in New York and there's work to be done. (Don Hamerman)

At about 3:45, the cry of "last call" can be heard in the more than 5,917 New York bars that are required by law to stop serving drinks at 4:00. Customers whose thirst has not quite been slaked by then may find their way to one of the hundreds of "bottle clubs" the state allows to exist if they are "non-profit, religious, fraternal or charitable organizations or duly recognized political clubs." The spirit of the law, which also defines a bottle club as a place that accommodates 100 or more people, is that no money may change hands between the drinkers and the persons who serve them.

But what if it's 3:30 in the morning, you don't want another drink, and you're still wide awake? If you're in the neighborhood of Lexington Avenue and 50th Street, you can stop by the Kaufman Pharmacy and pick up a package of Alka-Seltzer. It won't be a lonely experience. The all-night drug store does about 15 percent of its total nighttime business between 3:30 and 3:45, just before the bars close for the night. From there, it's just a hop, skip, and a jump to Lexington and 57th Street and the Rialto Florist; at that time of night there may be as many as 16 other people waiting in line, possibly for a dozen roses, Rialto's best-selling late-night item.

At 4:00 A.M. there are nearly 200 restaurants and coffee shops still open in Manhattan alone and possibly twice that many delicatessens. Two Manhattan Grand Union supermarkets are open all night, one in the Village and the other in Yorkville on the Upper East Side. Students of the singles scene say the Yorkville store is as important to the game they play as any bar in the neighborhood. Pathmark, a chain that keeps eight of its New York City supermarkets open 24 hours a day, boasts that there is never a time in any one of them that somebody isn't shopping for something.

But a lot more people than just hungry singles are out looking for food in the wee hours of the morning. Many restaurateurs go shopping immediately after they close their restaurants for the night. Their first stop might be the Hunt's Point Market in the South Bronx, which opens for business at about 4:00 in the morning and sells everything from apples and bananas to string beans and spinach. The pick of the crop goes to the first customers on the scene, and anyone getting there after 8:00 will probably leave empty-handed.

At about the same time the produce market begins its business day, at the Fulton Fish Market in downtown Manhattan they are unloading the day's catch. Between 4:00 and 8:00 on a typical morning, 6,000,000 pounds of fish will be sold. Located along the East River, where fishing boats docked a century ago to avoid the winter ice that plagued the Hudson River, the fish market is popular with late nighters and early risers looking for a touchstone with the past. Though today 99 percent of the catch comes by truck from as far north as Nova Scotia and as far south as

Louisiana, the 100 wholesalers who receive it are almost carbon copies of their grandfathers. They wear long green smocks and high hip boots, and they perch big curved hooks over their shoulders as they steer hand trucks over the wet pavement.

Many New Yorkers are not quite so energetic at 4:00 A.M., however. Many are home, relaxing, watching the late late movie, or calling other night people like themselves on the telephone. Some call friends. Others call the city's Poison Control Hotline—possibly to find out what to do after taking the wrong dose of medicine before going to bed. Still others may be on the line with the DiMele Center for Psychotherapy, which provides 24-hour help to people who need it. A call to the alcoholism hotline will explain why the hair of the dog that bit you is not a good idea for tomorrow morning. And if you're wondering if it might not be a better idea to just stay in bed all day tomorrow, a call to New York Telephone's Horoscopes-By-Phone might tell you if they're right.

Four o'clock in the morning is also a time when many people are making momentous decisions. Suddenly, at precisely 3:58 on the morning after his 42nd birthday, Howie Blum decided he wanted to get married. And he wanted to do it right away before he changed his mind. The legal entanglements of waiting periods and marriage licenses make that impossible, even in New York. Besides, Howie didn't know anybody who would marry him. But that part of his problem was easily solved. All Howie had to do was pick up the phone and dial Dan Field, the marriage broker. Dan is an old-world matchmaker who has gone his competition one better by instituting a 24-hour phone service that allows people like Howie to be interviewed at 4:00 in the morning and have a list of ten good prospects in his hands by the start of the next business day.

Within 90 days of his first phone call to Dan Field, Howie Blum did indeed get married. A confirmed sentimentalist, he scheduled the ceremony for 3:58 in the morning. After the wedding he and his bride, the former Sylvia Gold, checked in at the Plaza Hotel for what was left of the night. Traffic outside their window was light when they arrived, but before they got to bed it was increasingly noticeable. Morning was coming.

At that hour, at the 64 radio stations that serve the city, the people who act as Greater New York's wake-up service are checking with the weather bureau, updating their news reports, and sipping coffee to make sure they are really wide awake before they go on the air.

It's surprisingly easy to get a taxi at 5:00 in the morning. Cabbies do a big business in the morning rush hour, and many are on the streets early to get a head start. The fares they get are often headed for the all-night Art Deco diners and restaurants with a 1950s flavor popular with what one owner calls "the hip upbeat crowd" and another describes as "artists, bar people, and punk rockers." Call them what you will, these eateries are all dedicated to maintaining New York's reputation as a city that never sleeps, and they hold down the fort night after night until the truck drivers and other early risers arrive about 6 A.M.

Mike Shanahan is a trucker who likes to get his rig out of New York early. But he's never in too much of a hurry not to have a cup of coffee first. Mike's been an early morning regular in a West Side diner for more than 25 years. A few years ago the fashion crowd discovered the place, too. "I used to kid them about not modernizing this joint," says Mike. "Look at that coffee urn. Noah had one just like it on the ark! But these kids love it. They stand on line to get in here. I have to admit they've made the place more fun, though. They dress like I did when I was a kid. Except none of us guys ever dyed our hair pink. We didn't wear sequins or earrings, either. But that's progress, right? The only thing I don't get is why do these people wear sunglasses all the time? I bet some of them haven't seen the sun for weeks!"

Of course Mike is wrong. Really dedicated night people see the sun every day. And they see it at the best time of day: just as it's coming up in the morning. They share this event with joggers and dog walkers. They share it with tugboat crews in the harbor, with policemen ending their night tour, with apartment building superintendents who have their fingers crossed hoping no tenant will call to say there's no hot water. When the first light appears out over Long Island, inbound traffic is already at a standstill. As the light increases, the Fifth Avenue façade of the Empire State Building often turns to an indescribable shade of pink, accented by the only lights still burning in the tower, the flashing red lights of the TV antenna.

Even at sunrise the streets are full of pedestrians hurrying off to their jobs. There is work to be done. Night is less than 12 hours away.

The row of Greek Revival houses on the uptown side of Washington Square Park is one of the finest in the city. But they never look better than when their balustrades are decorated with new-fallen snow. (Matthew Klein)

Before it was a park, Washington Square was a parade ground. The passing parade there is still fascinating most nights, but a snowfall can cut the number of strollers down considerably. (André Kertesz)

Spacers to determine the configuration of 13 separate raised positions of the 3-ton contour curtain.

Dials to pre-set heights of the three stage elevators, up to 13 feet above the stage or 27 feet below.

Dials showing the actual positions of the 70-foot-wide stage elevators.

The backstage paging system.

Spacers to show the actual position of the contour curtain.

Elevator control switches.

Dial to show the position of the orchestra pit elevator.

Switches to pre-set the contour curtain or to activate each of the separate cables.

Master switch to raise or lower the 2,000-yard curtain.

The Backstage Engineer's Console at Radio City Music Hall

The Radio City Music Hall hydraulic stage elevators, installed when the Hall was built in 1932, were used as prototypes for the flight deck elevators in aircraft carriers and were classified as a military secret in the early years of World War II. The contour curtain is the largest theatrical curtain in the world and fills the 60 × 100' proscenium.